Sally

Lehrwerk für den
Englischunterricht ab Klasse 1

Activity Book 2

Erarbeitet von
Jasmin Brune
Daniela Elsner
Barbara Gleich
Stefanie Gleixner-Weyrauch
Simone Gutwerk
Marion Lugauer
Sabine Schwarz

unter Beratung von
Jane Brockmann-Fairchild

Illustriert von
Barbara Jung, Wilfried Poll,
Andreas Fischer und Gisela Vogel

Oldenbourg Schulbuchverlag, München

Draw lines. / Circle.
Number. / Write.

 Colour. / Draw.

 Cut.

 Stick.

 Point.

 Listen.

Say. / Tell. / Act out.

Play the game.

Sally's task

Lied/Reim auf Schüler-CD und Lehrer-CD

Geschichte/Hörtext nur auf Lehrer-CD

Redaktion: Salomé Dick, Berlin
Illustrationen: Barbara Jung, Wilfried Poll, Andreas Fischer und Gisela Vogel
Umschlagkonzept: Mendell & Oberer, München
Umschlagillustration: Barbara Jung
Layout: Lisa Neuhalfen, Berlin
Technische Umsetzung: Lisa Neuhalfen, Berlin

Tonaufnahmen: FLOEDL Audioproduktion, Ziemetshausen; Thomas Blendinger, Sommerhausen

www.cornelsen.de

1. Auflage, 7. Druck 2023

Alle Drucke dieser Auflage sind inhaltlich unverändert
und können im Unterricht nebeneinander verwendet werden.

© 2015 Cornelsen Schulverlag GmbH, Berlin
© 2016 Cornelsen Verlag GmbH, Berlin

Druck: Athesiadruck GmbH

ISBN 978-3-637-01964-5

PEFC-zertifiziert
Dieses Produkt
stammt aus
nachhaltig
bewirtschafteten
Wäldern

PEFC
PEFC/18-31-166   www.pefc.de

1 ✏️ Write.

2 🖍️ 🖌️ Stick in and colour.

3 💬 Tell.

1  Listen and colour.

2 Write.

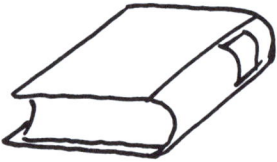  

schoolbag   **book**   **pencil case**

3 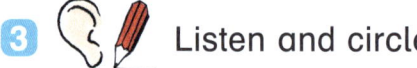 Listen and circle.

   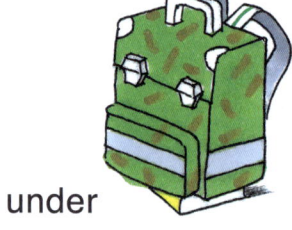   

in   under   on

on   in   under

in   under   on

6   CD 1.12

Sally 2 Activity Book © 2015 Cornelsen Schulverlage GmbH, Berlin

1 ✏️ Count and write.

2 💬 Tell.

1  Listen and number.

  **2** Create your dream school uniform. Present.
My school uniform is a … and a …

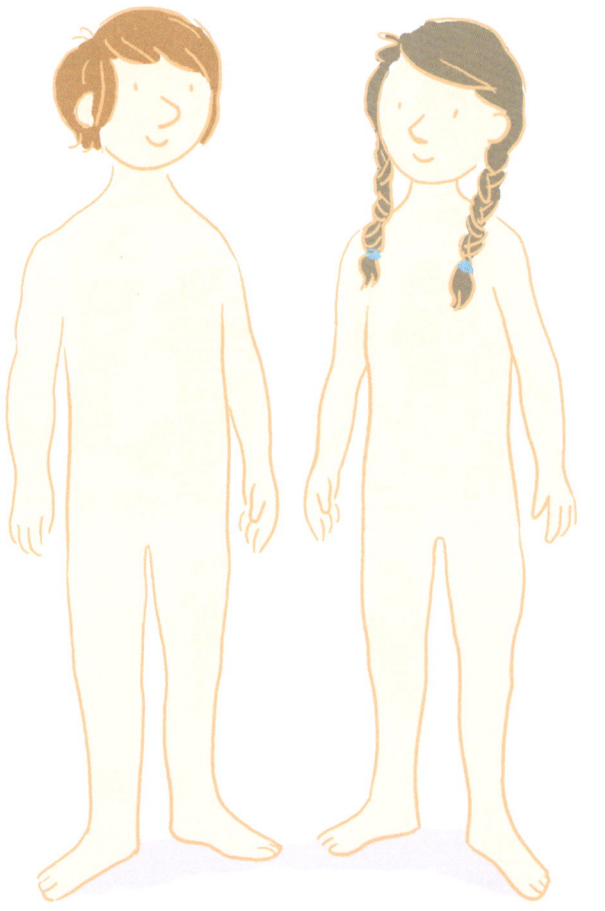

Sally 2 Activity Book © 2015 Cornelsen Schulverlage GmbH, Berlin

1  Listen and stick in.

① 	② 
③ 	④ 
⑤ 	⑥ 

2  Listen and write.

arms   feet

hands   legs

3 Colour.

CD 1.19

Sally 2 Activity Book © 2015 Cornelsen Schulverlage GmbH, Berlin

Body and clothes

1   Look, tell and write.

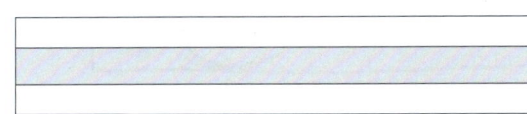

| shoes | T-shirt | skirt | trousers |

11

1 👂 🖌 Listen and draw.

2 ✏ Write.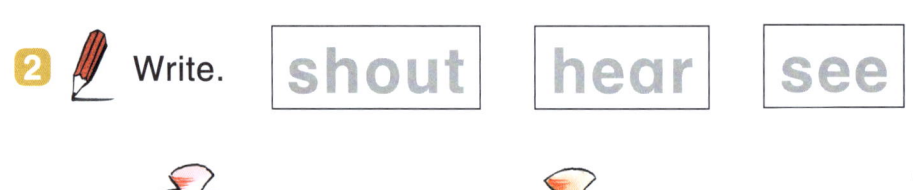

shout   hear   see

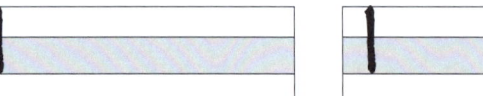  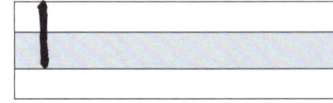

12   CD 1.25

1  Listen and number.

  **1** Listen and stick in.

1

2

3

4

5

14 CD 1.32

Sally 2 Activity Book © 2015 Cornelsen Schulverlage GmbH, Berlin

1 🖌️ 🖋️ Colour and write.

ball   gameboy   stickers

playing cards   inline skates

2 💬 Tell.

1 💬 What's missing? Tell.

2 🖌 Draw.

Sally 2 Activity Book © 2015 Cornelsen Schulverlage GmbH, Berlin

1   Write and say.

5, 10, _____, 20, _____, 30

2, _____, 6, _____, _____, 12, _____, _____, _____, 20

3, 6, 9, _____, 15, _____, _____, 24, _____, _____

13, 15, _____, 19, _____, _____, 25, _____, _____

30, 29, _____, 27, _____, _____, 24, _____, 22, _____, 20

30, 28, _____, _____, 22, _____, _____, 16, _____, _____, _____

2  Look and tell.

	2	3	4		6	7	8	9	
11		13	14	15			18	19	20
21	22		24	25	26	27		29	

3 Listen and colour.

1	2	3	4	5	6	7	8	9	10
11	12	13	14	15	16	17	18	19	20
21	22	23	24	25	26	27	28	29	30

1 Stick in.

2 Tell.

3 Draw lines and write.

lettuce   carrot   bean

 radish    cucumber    tomato

Sally 2 Activity Book © 2015 Cornelsen Schulverlage GmbH, Berlin

1  Listen and number.

2  Read and write.

Come and
help us!

3  Stick in and draw.

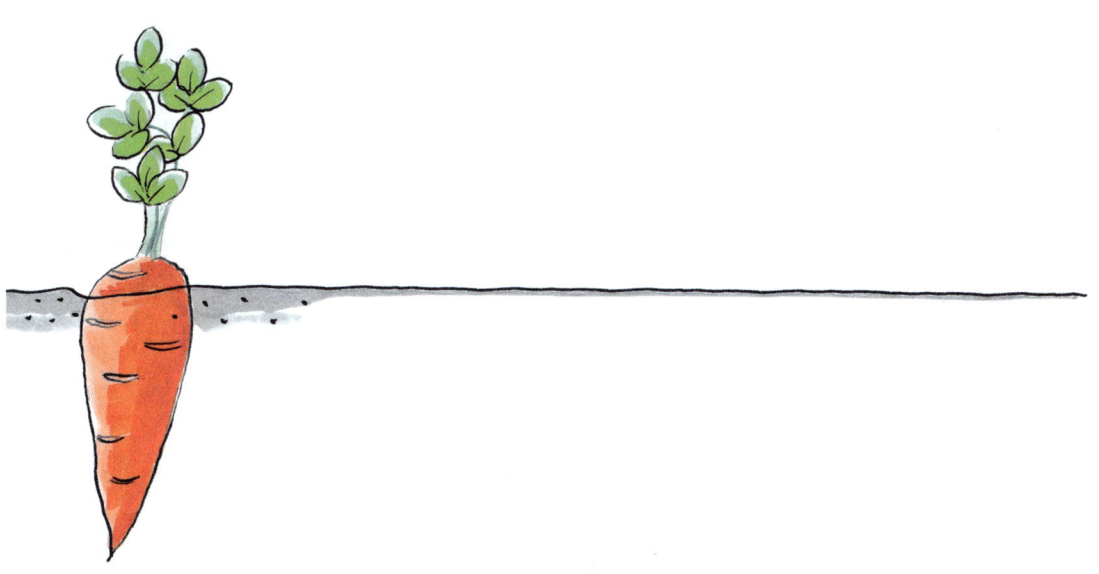

4 ⬭ Tell.

Sally 2 Activity Book © 2015 Cornelsen Schulverlage GmbH, Berlin

1 🖍 Read and write.

It's _____ . It's _____ .

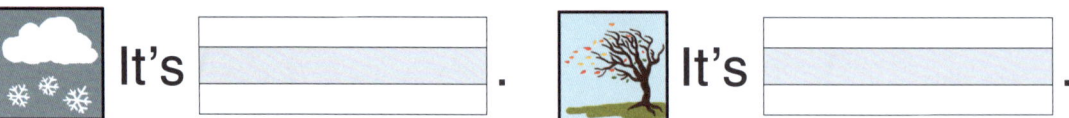

It's _____ . It's _____ .

| rainy | windy | sunny | snowy |

2 👂🖍 Listen and number.

3 🖍 Draw lines.

4 💬 Tell.

Sally 2 Activity Book © 2015 Cornelsen Schulverlage GmbH, Berlin

1  Point and count.

2  Listen and number.

3 Write.

  pig  hen  goose  duck

 horse  cow  sheep

1   Stick in.

2 Tell.

Sally 2 Activity Book © 2015 Cornelsen Schulverlage GmbH, Berlin

1 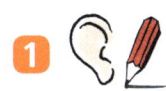  Listen and draw lines.

2 Write.

 frog  bat  spider

 **It's magic**

1  Write and draw the recipe.
Present.

Sally 2 Activity Book © 2015 Cornelsen Schulverlage GmbH, Berlin

1  Circle.

2  Colour and write.

Happy Halloween!

1 Listen and draw.

2 Write.

Merry Christmas!

3 Tell.

1  Listen and stick in.

1

2

3

4

5

6

Sally 2 Activity Book © 2015 Cornelsen Schulverlage GmbH, Berlin

CD 2.18

1 Play the game.

green   pink

orange   yellow   blue   red

blue yellow

red pink orange green

1 👂👉 Listen and point.   **2** 🖌 Colour and draw.

It's **autumn**.

It's **winter**.

3  Write.

It's spring.

It's summer.

Sally 2 Activity Book © 2015 Cornelsen Schulverlage GmbH, Berlin

1  Listen and stick in.

Sally 2 Activity Book © 2015 Cornelsen Schulverlage GmbH, Berlin

We're going on a bear hunt

1 🎲 Play the game.

We're going on a bear hunt

1 👂✏️ Listen and draw a line.

Sally 2 Activity Book © 2015 Cornelsen Schulverlage GmbH, Berlin

1 🎲 Play the game in your group.

It's ☁❄❄❄❄.

blue

book

11, 12, 13, ...

inline skates

hand

21, 22, 23, ...

Merry Christmas!

shoes

1

2

3

4

5

6

7

8

9

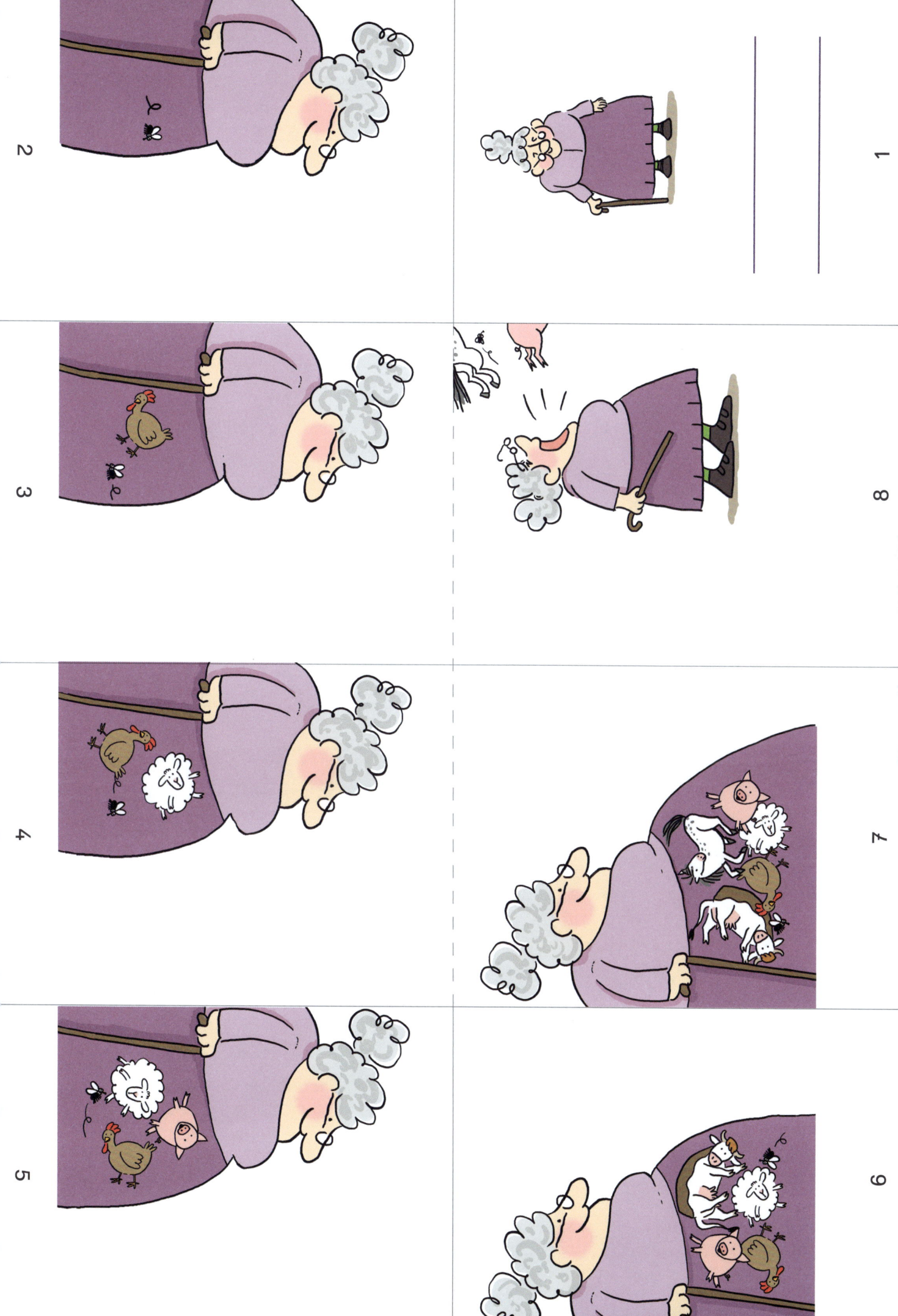

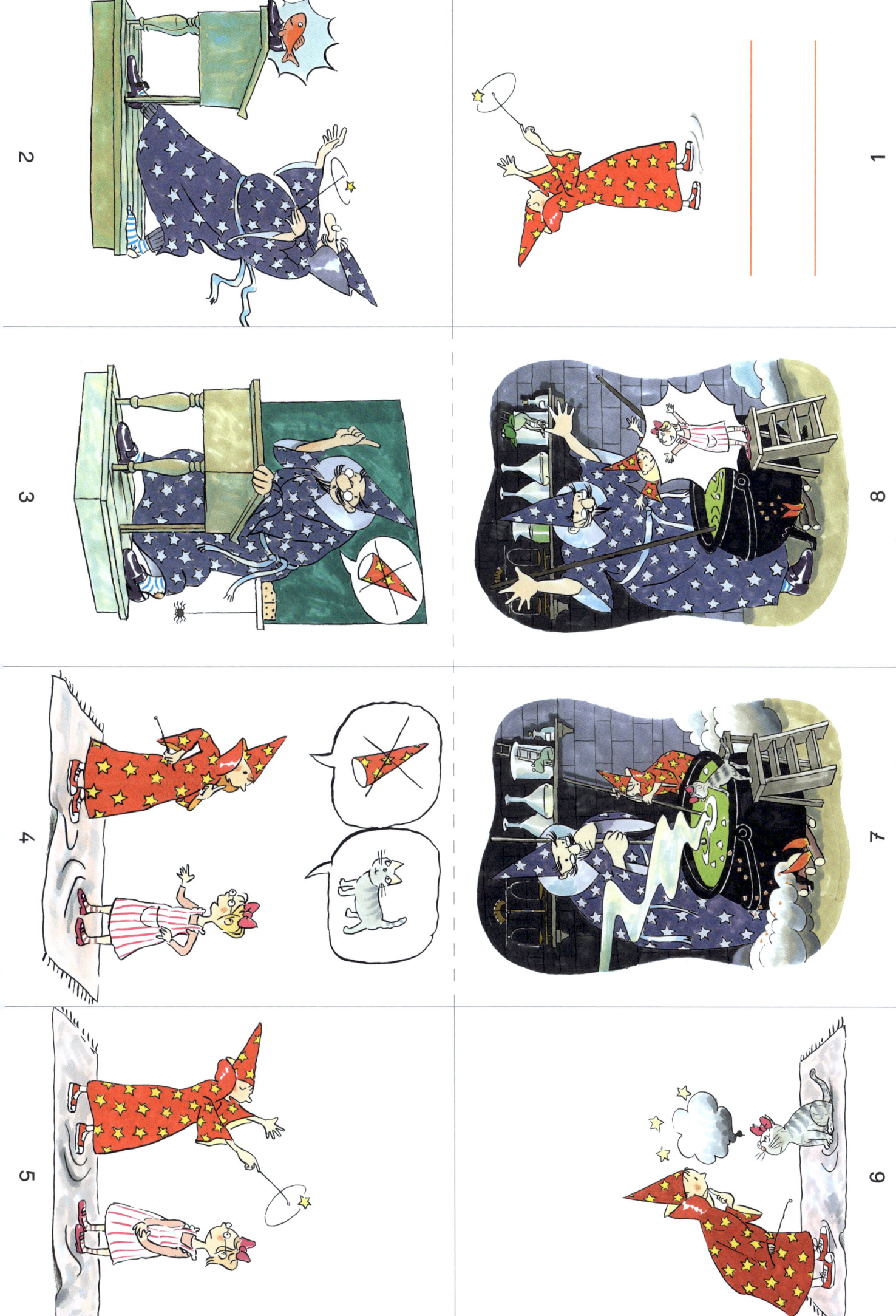